Overcoming
FEAR

Other Destiny Image Books
by Becky Dvorak

Conquering the Spirit of Death

*The Prophetic and Healing Power of
Your Words*

The Healing Creed

Greater Than Magic

Dare to Believe

BECKY DVORAK

Overcoming FEAR

Conquering the
SPIRIT OF FEAR
in Your Life

DESTINY IMAGE® PUBLISHERS, INC.
PO Box 310, Shippensburg, PA 17257-0310
"Promoting Inspired Lives"

This book and all other Destiny Image and Destiny Image Fiction books available at Christian bookstores and distributors worldwide.

For more information on foreign distributors, call 717-532-3040.

Or reach us on the Internet: www.destinyimage.com

ISBN 13 TP: 978-0-7684-5689-9

ISBN 13 ebook: 978-0-7684-5690-5

For Worldwide Distribution, Printed in the U.S.A.

1 2 3 4 5 6 / 24 23 22 21 20

Contents

The Negative Power of Fear

One of the negative emotions that partners with the spirit of death is fear. People fear many things such as bug, spiders, bats, snakes, darkness, lack of provision, being alone, rejection, germs, sickness and disease, and this list goes on and on—but the thing people fear more than the rest is death.

Inasmuch then as the children have partaken of flesh and blood, He Himself likewise shared in the same, that through death He might destroy him who had the power of death, that is, the devil, and release those who through fear of death were all their lifetime subject to bondage (Hebrews 2:14-15).

The Bible warns us that *"the thing I greatly fear has come upon me, and what I dreaded has happened to me"* (Job 3:25). Fear is a serious matter, and usually can be controlled. But when we allow it to fester within us, it becomes dangerous, and even deadly, as it works against us with a spirit of death.

This fear of death is very real, and it is more than a negative emotion—it's spiritual, and it's demonic. Second Timothy 1:7 says, *"For God has not given us a spirit of fear, but of power and of love and of a sound mind."* I have found during my many years in the healing ministry that a spirit of fear travels with sickness and disease. It is often the forerunner of a spirit of premature death. It takes a decision on the part of people who are gravely ill to not give into this spirit, and force themselves into the arena of faith where power, love, and a sound mind exist.

And Jesus more than anyone else understands this battle. In the Garden of Gethsemane, He knew He was about to be slaughtered for all people and that the suffering would be so torturous that He battled fear and sweat great drops of blood. (See Luke 22:41-44.) He was tempted to give up, but He overpowered this fear by faith and prayer. And this is how we will too.

I receive many prayer requests daily from God's people needing prayer for healing. They have received a very serious medical report and the fear of death has taken over their mind and emotions. But before the prayer of faith can take effect, this spirit of fear has to be dealt with.

Fear paralyzes the spiritual tongue, and then it affects the rest of the body. Why? In Proverbs 18:21 it says that life and death are in the power of the tongue. Your tongue possesses a power.

What is this power? It is the power of the spoken word. Words have the power to create or to destroy. This is why fear, first and foremost, paralyzes the healing power of the tongue. If you receive the injection of its venomous poison into your spirit, you will begin to speak failure, destruction, and even death. And by the power of your own tongue, what you speak will come to pass.

I know a young man who became very ill and was in a lot of pain. It was soon discovered that he had a cancerous tumor on his pancreas. He shared with me what happened to him when the doctors came into his hospital room to give him the bad medical report. He said that as he heard the death report, he could not speak. It was as if he had swallowed poison. What did he really swallow? He swallowed fear—more precisely a spirit of fear. He accepted this death report and a spirit of death entered into his spirit and immediately began to meditate and speak death.

It took others to speak words of hope and healing into his life in order for his faith to be encouraged to the point that he accepted the words of faith and started to speak them for himself. And once he started to speak faith-filled words of healing, health and life, his miracle manifested and the cancerous tumor disappeared, and it never came back.

It is of extreme importance that we protect ourselves from the spirit of death and refuse to accept its venomous poison—the spirit of fear.

Isaiah 41:10 (AMP) encourages us with these words: *"Do not fear [anything], for I am with you; Do not be afraid, for I am your God. I will strengthen you, be assured I will help you; I will certainly take hold of you with My righteous right hand [a hand of justice, of power, of victory, of salvation]."*

Four Scriptural Measures to Overcome Fear

1. **Set your thoughts on godly matters, instead of earthly ones.** Paul, an apostle of Jesus Christ, by the will of God writes to us in Colossian 3:2, instructing us to *"set your mind on things above, not on things on the earth."* Refuse to dwell on the negative reports and force your mind and emotions to focus on the promises of God. It may seem like false faith in the

beginning but you have to take this first initial step to transform fear into faith.

2. **Give your worries to God.** Peter, another apostle of Jesus Christ, in First Peter 5:7 encourages us with these words, *"Casting all your care upon Him, for He cares for you."* Ponder upon God's Word that He truly does love and care for you. And that He will faithfully see you through the situation.

3. **Pray in tongues and encourage yourself.** Again, the apostle Paul teaches us in First Corinthians 14:4 (NIV): *"Anyone who speaks in a tongue edifies themselves...."* When fear tries to overwhelm you, start to pray in tongues. Encourage yourself throughout the day and night by praying in your heavenly language— it works.

4. **Choose to think upon the positive promises of God.** Paul, also referred to as a bond-servant of Jesus Christ, writes to us in Philippians 4:8 (NIV): *"Finally, brothers and sisters, whatever is true, whatever is noble, whatever is right, whatever is pure whatever is lovely, whatever is admirable—if anything is excellent or praiseworthy—think about such things."* Choose what you think about. If it doesn't align itself to the message of this verse, to put it out of your mind.

Let's Pray

Call out to the Father right now and confess to Him your fears,

> *Father God, I am fearful that I will not ever feel well again, that my healing might not manifest. I feel insecure that I do not measure up to You and to others.*

I am afraid of being alone. Father, forgive me for taking in and sheltering this spirit of fear. Right now, by faith I am giving it an eviction notice and it must leave the premises of my temple now! Help me, Holy Spirit, to remember that I do not need to fear, that I am as bold as a lion, and more than a conqueror, in Jesus' name I pray, amen.

The As[...]

Spi[...]

To overcome fear we need to rid our mind and emotions of doubt and unbelief concerning the promises of God. And the cure for fear is the assurance of our spiritual rights. For too long we have allowed satan entrance into our soulish realm (our mind and emotions) and whisper his vicious lies that our Lord does not care about us, or that God is evil and waiting to set us up for harm. The devil trembles at the thought that we might receive this revelation that we have spiritual rights—and walk in assurance of them.

e suffering from broken
cial difficulties and incur-
s and diseases. They desire a
s touch from God and do not
and why it is not happening. They
e not been taught that they possess a
tle deed called "faith" that gives them covenant rights with the Father to make their
hopes a reality.

After ministering the Word of God at a
faith and healing conference, I was admin-
istering the healing power of God to those
standing in the healing line. I was pre-
sented to a woman who had been bound to
a wheelchair for many years. She was bit-
ter and angry with everyone, but mostly
at God. Her marriage was in ruins. Her
dream to be a mother was stolen from her.
Her financial situation looked impossible.
And she lost her desire to live.

As I went to lay my hand on her, she screamed out with all her might, "When God?" I knelt down and looked her in the eye and said, "God is not withholding your miracle from you. This tragedy in your life is not of God, but of satan. Right now, we are going to take our authority over satan and all of his wicked works and release God's healing power into your body. Then, we are going to put our faith in action and you will walk again."

The Assurance

How could I be so sure that God was going to heal this woman? Because I know God, and His Word says in First John 3:8b about Jesus, *"For this purpose the Son of God was manifested, that He might destroy the works of the devil,"* and Hebrews 13:20 speaks of the everlasting covenant we have with the Father: *"Now may the God of peace who brought up our Lord Jesus from the dead, the great Shepherd of the sheep, through the blood of the everlasting covenant."*

This everlasting covenant we have with our heavenly Father is our title deed that states in First John 5:14-15, *"Now this is the confidence that we have in Him, that if we ask anything according to His will, He hears us. And if we know that He hears us, whatever we ask, we know that we have the petitions that we have asked of Him."*

A title deed is a legal document that has been signed, sealed and delivered that lawfully transfers property to a new owner and verifies that person's legal right to possess it.

Hebrews 11:1, in the Amplified Bible, says, *"Now faith is the assurance (the confirmation, the title deed) of the things [we] hope for, being the proof of things [we] do not see and* the conviction of their reality [faith perceiving as real fact what is not revealed to the senses]." Faith is our title deed; we are the rightful owners of those things we are hoping for.

What is it that we are hoping for? Are we hoping for physical healing? Our title deed states in Jeremiah 30:17a, "'For I will restore health to you, and heal you of your wounds,' says the Lord." Are we hoping for a restored marriage? It is written in Matthew 19:26, *"But Jesus looked at them and said to them, 'With men this is impossible, but with God all things are possible.'"* Are we hoping for a better job that can support the needs of your family? Philippians 4:19 promises us, *"And my God shall supply all your need according to His riches in glory by Christ Jesus."*

The woman who was bound to a wheelchair, whose marriage was in ruins, whose dream to have a child was lost, was in need of a title deed called "faith" in order to make her hopes a reality.

She received this assurance of her spiritual rights found in this free title deed and now walks; her marriage is restored, she has given birth to a child, and her financial situation is better than it was before.

We too need this assurance that we have legal, spiritual rights to possess our hopes; trust in God's goodness and grace to honor His Word—our title deed of faith.

Are you ready to overcome fear and rid your mind and emotions of doubt and unbelief concerning the promises of God? And will you do what it takes to access the assurance of your legal spiritual rights to possess your much-needed miracle?

The Empowerment
of the Spirit

In order to walk free from fear and in the realm of the miraculous, we need to align ourselves with Holy Spirit. The Holy Spirit is the creative, explosive power of God. The miraculous is His realm. The Holy Spirit lives and resides within the spirit of every believer in Jesus Christ. When we are baptized in the Holy Spirit, we give Him permission to manifest His power in our lives. It's like lighting a match. That matchstick already has the sulfur to produce fire, but until something strikes that match that fire-producing power cannot be released.

And so it is like this simple visual when we are baptized in the Holy Spirit, and His creative, explosive power is released in us.

This baptism of Holy Spirit is a very powerful spiritual weapon that God has given to us to overcome the attacks of the enemy. I believe this is why satan has caused so much division within the Body of Christ concerning it. But regardless of the division, His Word is truth.

The Power of Praying in Tongues

One night, in the year of 2000 at our children's home in Guatemala, something supernatural happened that as long as I live I will never forget, and forever solidified within me the importance of praying in tongues.

My son Aaron and I were at home with all the children, and one of the boys had a problem with drug addiction and demon possession. I don't know what he had done that night, but I think he had taken some type of drug or chemical.

It was nighttime, and the electricity went out; and we could all literally sense a very evil presence in the atmosphere. Suddenly, something became seriously wrong with this boy. We started calling him; he was barely breathing. I activated my authority in Christ and commanded his spirit to start calling out the name of Jesus. Within a minute or two I could see that his tongue began to move, and we could hear him repeating under his breath, "Jesus, Jesus, Jesus…" Then the electricity came back on.

I looked him in the eye, and I could see with the discerning of spirits (see 1 Cor. 12:10) that he was still under the influence of demonic spirits. I knew we were in for another spiritual battle. I asked one of the older boys in the home to start reading from the Scriptures aloud. Then my son and I went to tend to the younger boys in the home. And yes, they were filled with fear at what they had seen and heard taking place.

The electricity went out again, and this boy started screaming and going wild, and wrapped himself up in a blanket trying to hide and escape from the situation. I ran into the room and started to rebuke this demonic stronghold over him. I asked, "In Jesus' name, who are you?" Immediately, I started to hear many voices talking at the same time, but they were not inside the room, or inside the house. They were outside of the house, actually surrounding the house. It sounded like thousands of voice all talking at once.

Suddenly, Aaron, who also walks in the gift of discerning of spirits,, ran into the room and shouted, "Mom, they (the demonic spirits) are surrounding the house! They are looking in the windows, some are flying, while others are wrapping chains around the house!"

We both started to pray in tongues and fight what was coming against us. The boy was screaming and totally out of control. We continued to pray fervently in tongues, when all of a sudden the presence of Holy Spirit overshadowed us and the present situation. We looked at each other and both busted out into laughter. We laughed so hard that tears were streaming from our eyes and we had to hold onto our bellies because it literally hurt to laugh that hard. As we continued to laugh uncontrollably, all the demons started to flee as fast as they could! And by the power of Holy Spirit, we laughed in the face of fear and called his bluff, and it was over. And we won this battle by the empowerment of Holy Spirit with the evidence of praying in tongues.

Scriptural Proof for the Baptism of Holy Spirit

I believe a clear biblical presentation about this baptism of Holy Spirit with the evidence of praying in tongues is necessary. After reading through this Bible study then we will pray.

In the book of Acts before Jesus ascended into heaven He was teaching the apostles about things to come. He told them of another baptism, the baptism of the Holy Spirit that would soon come upon them, (see Acts 1:5). He told them they would receive power when the Holy Spirit came upon them, (see Acts 1:8).

And in the second chapter of Acts we read of the Day of Pentecost when suddenly a noise came from heaven like a violent rushing wind and it filled the whole house, and tongues of fire rested upon them and they were all filled with the Holy Spirit and began to speak with other tongues, as the Spirit was giving the utterance. (See Acts 2:1-4.)

Most Christians believe that this took place, but many believe that mighty move of the Holy Spirit was for the early Church and not for believers today. Let's look to the Scriptures for clarity.

The Apostle Peter declared to the onlookers of this amazing event, starting with verse 14 that what they witnessed is what the Prophet Joel prophesied about, saying that in the last days a mighty outpouring of the Holy Spirit would come forth on all people. Did the world end with the early Church? No. This was referring to a new dispensation of the Holy Spirit, which did not end, but just began.

Peter continues to teach and tells the listeners what they need to do in verse 38. He tells them they need to repent, be baptized in the name of Jesus Christ for the forgiveness of sins, and that they will receive the gift of the Holy Spirit. And he goes on to tell them in the next verse who the promise of the Holy Spirit is for. He says to them, "For the promise is to you and to your children, and to all who are afar off, as many as the Lord our God will call" (see Acts 2:39). Peter includes us when he says, "and to all who are afar off" in the promise to receive the gift of the Holy Spirit.

Now, that we laid the foundation, let's continue on and see what else the Word has to say about the baptism of the Holy Spirit, tongues and the interpretation of tongues.

The Holy Spirit:

The Holy Spirit is a good gift from the Father, and not an evil one. It says in Luke 11:11-14, *"If a son asks for bread from any father among you, will he give him a stone? Or if he asks for a fish, will he give him a serpent instead of a fish? Or if he asks for an egg, will he offer him a scorpion? If you then, being evil, know how to give good gifts to your children, how much more will your heavenly Father give the Holy Spirit to those who ask Him?"*

The Baptism of the Holy Spirit:

The baptism of the Holy Spirit is powerful and reserved for the believer in Jesus Christ only. It would literally destroy an unregenerated spirit. It says in Luke 5:37-38, *"And no one puts new wine into old wineskins; or else the new wine will burst the wineskins and be spilled, and the wineskins will be ruined. But new wine must be put into new wineskins, and both are preserved."*

This baptism is for any and all believers in Jesus Christ. *"For the promise is to you and to your children, and to all who are afar off, as many as the Lord our God will call."* (Acts 2:39).

Through His baptism we receive His power, Acts 1:8 says, *"But you shall receive power when the Holy Spirit has come upon you; and you shall be witnesses to Me in Jerusalem, and in all Judea and Samaria, and to the end of the earth."*

The initial evidence of being baptized in the Holy Spirit is that you will pray in tongues. As it happens in Acts 2:4, *"And they were all filled with the Holy Spirit and began to speak with other tongues, as the Spirit gave them utterance."*

Tongues and the Interpretation of Tongues:

Tongues and its co-partner, the Interpretation of Tongues are spiritual gifts given to us by the Holy Spirit, and not the devil. (See 1 Corinthians 12:10.)

The Purpose of the Gift of Tongues:

The Holy Spirit prays through us when we don't know how. *"Likewise the Spirit also helps in our weaknesses. For we do not know what we should pray for as we ought, but the*

Spirit Himself makes intercession for us with groanings which cannot be uttered. Now He who searches the hearts knows what the mind of the Spirit is, because He makes intercession for the saints according to the will of God" (Rom. 8:26-27).

Our spirit prays for the unknown. *"For he who speaks in a tongue does not speak to men but to God, for no one understands him; however, in the spirit he speaks mysteries"* (1 Cor. 14:2).

To build ourselves up. *"He who speaks in a tongue edifies himself, but he who prophesies edifies the church"* (1 Cor. 14:4).

So supernatural power can flow through us. *"He who believes in Me, as the Scripture has said, out of his heart will flow rivers of living water"* (John 7:38).

The Purpose for the Interpretation of Tongues:

When we are in a public setting we need the gift of Interpretation of Tongues to be in operation so that the supernatural message can be understood by all. First Corinthians 14:13 gives us instruction concerning this situation, *"Therefore let him who speaks in a tongue pray that he may interpret."*

Prayer for the Baptism of Holy Spirit

Before we pray, here are some instructions to read through and then we will pray for this gift.

- Lay your hand upon your heart.

- Ask the Father for the baptism of Holy Spirit in the name of Jesus.

- Just like anything else, you need to put your faith into action. So, open up your mouth and start to move your tongue like you are about to speak, and expect to pray in tongues. The Holy Spirit will not force you to pray in tongues; you need to give voice to what you sense stirring within you. You need to cooperate with Holy Spirit. It's easy to do, but as you will learn—it's a very powerful supernatural weapon.

Dear Holy Spirit,

I am a believer in Jesus Christ, and I ask You in His name for this baptism of the Holy Spirit with the evidence of praying in tongues. In Jesus' name, amen.

Now open up your mouth, start to move your tongue, and give voice to what is starting to stir in your heart. It won't be anything you recognize. But do not be afraid; just cooperate with Holy Spirit. In time you will learn the importance and the power of this type of prayer.

Knowing Our True Identity in Christ

To walk fearlessly as we ought to, we need to know our true identity in Christ. Our true identity in Christ is probably the most important truth that satan tries to conceal from us because he knows that once we start to unveil this truth about who we really are in Christ and who Christ is in us, we become lethal to satan and his kingdom of darkness.

Once we start to recognize who we are in Christ we start to seize our authority over satan, the temptation of sin, and the consequences of living in a fallen world, such as sickness, disease, and every other foul curse that comes our way. In other words, we start to dominate satan and his evil works, instead of him controlling us. It is amazing that satan can identify those who start to comprehend their identity and operate in their authority in Christ.

I remember traveling to the Maasailand in Northern Tanzania for the first time. Before an evening evangelistic campaign, a demon-possessed man that I had never met or even heard of before ran out from the darkness to me and knelt down at my feet. The demons within him cried out to me in English (for I did not understand the local language), "Why have you come to torment us?" And got up and ran back into the wilderness. I was astounded that they could perceive when we know who we are in Christ. I believe it is partly by watching how we start to speak and act. And then I believe there is some sort of unveiling that takes place and when they look at us they see Jesus in us. And at this point, they have no other option but to yield to and admit defeat.

There were other Christians standing around me, even other Christian leaders, but the demon spirits in this man paid no attention, but instead cried out to the one who started to see who she was in Christ.

The understanding of our true identity in Christ is of utmost importance. Many Christians do not know who they are in Christ. They have not been taught that they are created in the mirror image of the Father, Son and Holy Spirit, and they are oblivious to their spiritual rank—"a little lower than Elohim." (See Psalm 8:5-6.) Therefore, they do not enforce their

God-given authority in which they are to walk in while on this earth.

"Behold, I give you the authority to trample on serpents and scorpions, and over all the power of the enemy, and nothing shall by any means hurt you" (Luke 10:19). Believers in Christ who lack this revelation take a passive stance against the enemy, and they rarely walk in the victory that they were created for. This is exactly what satan desires, passive, lukewarm Christians who walk in daily defeat.

Does satan have you hoodwinked so that he and others cannot see Christ within you? It's time to lift the veil of truth and see who you really are. Listen to what the Word of God says concerning you.

You are of God, little children, and have overcome them, because He who is in you is greater than he who is in the world (1 John 4:4).

Love has been perfected among us in this: that we may have boldness in the day of judgement; because as He is, so are we in this world (1 John 4:17).

Brethren, the Greater One in us is Jesus Christ, and as He is, so are we in this world. Jesus Christ is all-powerful over satan and all of his wicked works, and because of the redeeming power of the Blood of Jesus, we too are all-powerful over satan and over all of his wicked works. The more time we abide in this truth the clearer this revelation will become to us. And more importantly, the more we win over our enemy, that serpent of old.

Decree of Faith to Overcome a Spirit of Fear

The last point that I want to share with you to overcome a spirit of fear has to do with the use of your tongue and God's words, specifically, speaking about the use of decreeing God's Word to separate yourself from a spirit of fear.

What Is a Decree?

The word decree is Hebrew is *gazar*, and it means "to cut, to divide, or to separate" (Strong's H1504). And this is what happens in the spirit realm when we decree something. Job 22:28 (KJV) says, *"Thou shalt also decree a thing, and it shall be established unto thee: and the light shall shine upon thy paths."*

In Genesis 1:4, God decrees a separation between the light and the darkness: *"And God saw the light, that it was good; and God divided the light from the darkness."* In this instance, Strong's H914 matches the Hebrew word *badal*, and it means "to separate, distinguish, differ, divide as in asunder, make a separation."

We see the usage of this concept throughout creation as far as dividing the waters from the waters, the firmament from waters, and day from night. We also see it in Exodus 26:33, where God gives instructions to hang a veil to divide or to separate the holy place from the Most Holy. In Leviticus 10:10, this word is used to distinguish the difference between holy and unholy, clean and unclean. Isaiah 59:2 talks about iniquities separating us from the face of our God. There are many examples of the usage of this Hebrew word *badal* in the Word, and it means "to separate or to divide something from another, whether physically or spiritually."

When we decree a thing, we use the Word of God to separate ourselves, our families, our health, etc. from the power of negative reports filled with danger, sickness, death, poverty, or any other form of the curse.

In Exodus 14:15-16, when God commands Moses to lift up his rod and stretch out his hand over the Red Sea and divide it, not only does He make a supernatural passageway for the Israelites to cross over, but He creates and decrees a divider of protection between them and harm's way of

49

Pharaoh and his evil men pursuing them in verses 13-14:

> *And Moses said to the people, "Do not be afraid. Stand still, and see the salvation of the Lord, which He will accomplish for you today. For the Egyptians whom you see today, you shall see again no more forever. The Lord will fight for you, and you shall hold your peace."*

Let's look at a biblical example of a verbal decree to divide the godly from the ungodly. In Joshua 24:15, Joshua decrees over his family, *"...As for me and my house, we will serve the Lord."* Joshua verbally creates a divider, a spiritual boundary or wall between those who serve the Lord and those who don't. And He decrees that His family will serve God.

We separate ourselves from sickness and disease when we decree God's healing promise that "by His stripes we are healed." During a recent healing seminar in Ocala, Florida, a woman stepped forward for her healing. She had a bad fall that severely damaged seven of her discs, three in her neck and four in her lower back area, and the fall caused all of her nerves in her right shoulder to be pinched. She went to the doctor, and received shots to help with the pain. She said the shots helped a little but not much. She could not lift her arm or bend over. And she struggled to sleep at night because of the pain. She was scheduled for neck, back, and shoulder surgery within a month, but something supernatural happened instead. She said she heard about the healing seminar for two weeks and made up her mind to attend. That entire weekend she heard the healing word being decreed over her and everyone who attended the services.

Sunday morning she came forward, and I decreed that, "by His stripes you are healed." I told her to put her faith into action and do what she was not able to do before. She started to move her neck, and she said her neck cracked about seven times, and those of us who were near her heard the last crack. It was so loud that the crowd all wowed at the same time. Instantly the woman was completely healed. She regained total movement in both her arms, she could bend and squat and do things she had not been able to do in a number of years—all because we believed and decreed and she aligned her faith to the healing decree and her physical healing manifested the moment she believed.

Decrees are based on the Word of God and produce in the physical realm what they are verbally sent out to do. Now let's use this spiritual principle of decreeing to help overcome a spirit of fear.

A Decree of Faith to Confess to Overcome a Spirit of Fear

I decree that God has not given me a spirit of fear, but of power and of love and of a sound mind, Second Timothy 1:7. I am strong and courageous, I am not afraid, or dismayed, for the Lord my God is with me wherever I go, Joshua 1:9. I am established in righteousness, far from oppression, I will not fear; terror shall not come near me, Isaiah 54:14. The peace of God, which surpasses all understanding, guards my heart and mind through Christ Jesus, Philippians 4:7.

I set my mind on things above, to on things on the earth, Colossians 3:2. And whatever things are true, whatever things are noble, whatever things are just, whatever things are pure, whatever things are lovely, whatever things are of good report, if there is any virtue and if there is anything praiseworthy—I meditate on these things, Philippians 4:8.

I am strong and courageous, I am not afraid, or dismayed, for the Lord my God is with me wherever I go, Joshua 1:9. I am bold as a lion, Proverbs 28:1. I have the authority to trample on serpents and scorpions, and over all the power of the enemy, and nothing shall by any means hurt me, Luke 10:19.

The Lord is on my side; I will not fear. What can man to do me? Psalm 118:6. God is for me, so who can be against me? Romans 8:31. The Lord is my light and my salvation; whom shall I fear? The Lord is the strength of my life; of whom shall be afraid? Psalm 27:1.

Jesus' peace is with me, He gave His peace to me; He does not give as the world gives. My heart will not be troubled, and I will not let it be afraid, John 14:27. I will fear not, for God is with me; I will not be dismayed, for He is my God. He will strengthen me, yes, He will help me, He will uphold me with His righteous right hand, Isaiah 41:10.

Therefore, I do not worry about tomorrow, for tomorrow will worry about its own things. Sufficient for the day is its own trouble, Matthew 6:34. I cast all my care upon Him, for He cares for me, First Peter 5:7.

For I am persuaded that neither death nor life, or angels nor principalities or powers, nor things present nor things to come, nor height nor depth, nor any other created thing, shall be able to separate me from the love of God, which is in Christ Jesus my Lord, Romans 8:38-39.

I sought the Lord, and He heard me, and delivered me from all my fears, Psalm 34:4.

In Jesus' name I declare these promises of God over myself, amen.

Pray this decree of faith over yourself aloud as often as you need to, and allow this decree to build a separation between you and a spirit of fear.

About the Author

BECKY DVORAK, author of *DARE to Believe*, *Greater Than Magic*, *The Healing Creed*, *The Prophetic and Healing Power of Your Words*, and content partner with Spirit Led Woman / Charisma, is a prophetess and healing evangelist who conducts healing services, seminars, and conferences globally. After being full-time missionaries since 1994 with her husband David in Guatemala, Central America, Becky now resides in the United States. Becky and David are the founders of Healing and Miracles International, Vida Ilimitada, and Life Tender Mercy Children's Home. They celebrate 39 years of marriage, have 8 children, 3 biological, 5 adopted, 1 son-in-law, 5 daughters-in-law, and 10 grandchildren.

Made in the USA
Las Vegas, NV
15 August 2024

93823519R00037